Did Yo

ISLE OF

A MISCELLANY

Compiled by Julia Skinner

With particular reference to the work of John Bainbridge,
Valerie McGee and Adrian Searle

THE FRANCIS FRITH COLLECTION

www.francisfrith.com

First published in the United Kingdom in 2012 by The Francis Frith Collection®

This edition published exclusively for Identity Books in 2012 ISBN 978-1-84589-683-6

British Library Cataloguing in Publication Data

Did You Know? Isle of Wight - A Miscellany
Compiled by Julia Skinner
With particular reference to the work of John Bainbridge, Valerie McGee and Adrian Searle

The Francis Frith Collection
Oakley Business Park,
Wylye Road, Dinton,
Wiltshire SP3 5EU
Tel: +44 (0) 1722 716 376
Email: info@francisfrith.co.uk
www.francisfrith.com

Printed and bound in Malaysia
Contains material sourced from responsibly managed forests

Front Cover: **COWES, THE FLOATING BRIDGE 1913** 66313p
Frontispiece: **GODSHILL, THE VILLAGE AND CHURCH 1913** 66173
Contents: **VENTNOR, FROM THE CLIFFS 1918** 68280

The colour-tinting is for illustrative purposes only, and is not intended to be historically accurate

AS WITH ANY HISTORICAL DATABASE, THE FRANCIS FRITH ARCHIVE IS CONSTANTLY BEING CORRECTED AND IMPROVED, AND THE PUBLISHERS WOULD WELCOME INFORMATION ON OMISSIONS OR INACCURACIES

CONTENTS

INTRODUCTION

The shape of the Isle of Wight resembles a rough-cut diamond, appropriately for this jewel of England's south coast, a few miles offshore from the Hampshire mainland. The Isle of Wight was part of Hampshire from Anglo-Saxon times until 1890, when it became an independent administrative county in its own right.

The Island is famous for its mild climate, spectacular coastal scenery, coloured cliffs, a verdant landscape of patchwork fields and hedgerows, high downlands, deep wooded valleys and dramatically scenic chines – short, steep valleys that slice through the southern landscape, densely-wooded and thick with ferns. Almost dividing the Island in two is the lengthy River Medina, which empties into the sea at Cowes.

Before the advent of popular tourism in the 19th century, most people on the Island made their living in traditional trades like fishing, farming and shipbuilding. It was Queen Victoria who made the Isle of Wight a fashionable holiday destination for hundreds of thousands of her subjects. In her childhood she had spent several holidays on the Island and formed a fondness for it. After her marriage to Prince Albert she bought Osborne House on the Island, using it as her favoured winter retreat until the very end of her life. The consequences of that royal patronage changed the Island for ever. Fishing villages became residential towns and important resorts, the population soared and towns enjoyed a housing boom as residences and hotels were built to cater for the increased demand for homes. Many of the archive photographs in this book were taken when the Island's holiday industry was in its Victorian heyday, but tourism is still of vital importance to the Island's economy, with over 2.5 million visitors coming to the Isle of Wight each year. That this tourism industry has developed to this extent over the years without seriously compromising the very beauty of the Island that all those tourists still come to see is surely a credit not only to those who lived and worked on Wight during those important formative years, but also to those who are its custodians today.

The Isle of Wight had an important part in the defence of the ports of Southampton and Portsmouth in past centuries, guarding both the eastern and western approaches to the Solent. There are many relics of castles, forts and batteries on the Island, some dating from Tudor times, although the guns seen in the photograph below were never used to defend Wight – they are part of a row of twenty-one cannon stationed at the Royal Yacht Squadron's headquarters, which are used to start the yachting races during Cowes Week each August, one of the most important events in the Island's calendar. They were originally the guns of the sailing ship 'Royal Adelaide', which belonged to King William IV (1830-37). Even so, this photograph is a good illustration of several roles the Isle of Wight has played over the centuries – from defensive stronghold to yachting mecca and holiday paradise, with the Red Funnel ferry 'Vecta' coming into Cowes harbour in the background, full of passengers eagerly looking forward to a wonderful holiday.

COWES, THE 'VECTA' AND THE CANNON OF THE ROYAL YACHT SQUADRON c1955 C173038

ISLE OF WIGHT DIALECT WORDS

The Isle of Wight dialect which was characterised by elongated vowels ('home' pronounced 'hooam' for example) has, inevitably, largely disappeared. Some specific Island words do survive in fairly common use, however. Islanders still refer to their mid-morning snack as ***'nammet',*** a word which one interpretation says derives from 'noon-meat', whilst another theory is that it comes from the traditional bread and cheese eaten at this time of day with strong beer – a snack containing no meat, hence ***'nammet'***.

'Grockles' – tourists.

'Grockle-can' – a tour coach.

'Overners' – incomers, ie people who have come over from the mainland to live and settle on the Island.

'Nipper' or ***'nips'*** – a boy, or young man.

'Mallishag' – a caterpillar.

'Gallybagger' – a scarecrow.

'Bugle' – a young bull.

'Caulkhead' – a term used for people who were born on the Island, although some people hold that to qualify as a true caulkhead, and a real Islander, your parents and grandparents also need to have been Wight-born. The name is believed to derive from the process of caulking boats to make them waterproof by sealing joints and seams with fibrous material, and is thus a reference to the Island's important boat building and boat repair industries of the past.

HAUNTED ISLE OF WIGHT

The Isle of Wight is said to be the most haunted island in the world, so much so that is has earned the title 'Ghost Island'! Here are just a few of the spooky tales about the Island's haunted places:

God's Providence House in Newport, now a tea room and restaurant (see page 19), may have a resident ghost in the shape of a little girl who has been seen in one of the dining rooms.

One of the Island's famous haunted places is the shell of the 18th-century Appuldurcombe House at Wroxall, near Ventnor, once one of Wight's great houses. It was hit by a parachuted German land mine in the Second World War, and is now a partially restored romantic ruin of baroque elegance in the care of English Heritage. Several unquiet shades are said to haunt Appuldurcombe, including ghostly brown-clad monks and a crying baby, and a phantom carriage parks outside the front entrance of the house.

Another of the Island's great houses of the past was Knighton Gorges, near Newchurch, but only the weathered stone gateposts of the entrance to the house remain today, supposedly haunted by the ill-starred Dillington family who lived there in earlier times. A ghostly coach-and-four is said to pass through the gateway, and the unquiet shade of Sir Tristram Dillington rides his horse through the gateway of his former home on the anniversary of his death by suicide on 7th July 1721. The gateposts are reputed to be the most haunted place on the Island, and it is said that if you go there on New Year's Eve you will see the now-demolished house of Knighton Gorges appear in ghostly form, and hear the sound of music, laughter and revelry coming from inside the spectral mansion…

ISLE OF WIGHT MISCELLANY

Wight became an island 8-9,000 years ago, at the end of the last Ice Age. Meltwater caused heightened sea levels, resulting in the sea's demolition of the massive chalk ridge that linked the Island to mainland Britain. The narrow barrier between the old Solent river and the sea was breached by rising waters, allowing the sea to pour into the western Solent between Wight and what is now Dorset, joining the river flowing down present-day Southampton Water into the sea via the channel of the eastern Solent. At either end of the gap in the chalk, the chalk stacks in the sea known as Old Harry Rocks at Swanage in east Dorset and The Needles at Alum Bay off the Isle of Wight are all that remain of that chalk ridge. Despite their name, there is nothing very thin and sharply pointed about any of the three chalk stacks making up The Needles nowadays. The one stack that did resemble the sewing implement – the Needle Rock itself – fell into the sea in 1764. The gap it left is seen in the photograph on the opposite page.

Alum Bay at the western point of Wight is famous for its coloured cliffs as well as The Needles, where blue, red, yellow, grey, white and black shades of strata are arranged vertically down the cliff face; they were created by water percolating through the surface over thousands of years, depositing chemicals that have coloured the sandstone. You are forbidden – for your own good as well as the coastline's – from clambering over the cliffs in search of a particular hue, but you can buy the coloured sand in a variety of decorated glass containers.

In 1897 the pioneering Italian inventor Guglielmo Marconi, 'father of long distance radio transmission', crowned earlier land-to-ship experiments on the Isle of Wight coast by setting up the first wireless telegraph station in the world on the cliffs above Alum Bay. In 1898 the first paid Marconigram – an early form of telegram – was transmitted from this station. Appropriately, the Island is now the home of the National Wireless Museum, at Puckpool Park, east of Ryde.

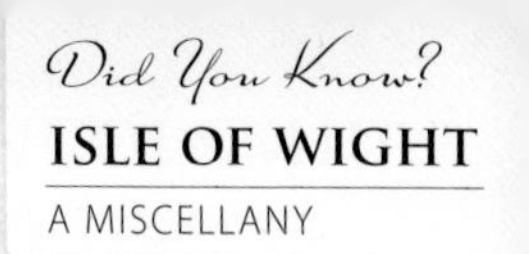

The Needles and Alum Bay are near the village of Freshwater, where Farringford, now a hotel, was the home in the 19th century of Alfred, Lord Tennyson (1809-1892), the Victorian Poet Laureate, who moved there in 1853. He loved to walk on the downs around Freshwater Bay, and High Down was renamed Tennyson Down in his honour after his death. His memorial stands there today. From it, the views across the Western Solent recall his famous poem 'Crossing the Bar', in which he expressed his thoughts as he contemplated death and what lay beyond, reputedly written whilst Tennyson crossed the 'bar' of the Western Solent to the Island on the Lymington-Yarmouth ferry.

An unusual fact about the Solent, the strait of water between the Hampshire coast and the Isle of Wight, is that it has four tides a day, with two high tide peaks, a phenomenon known as 'Double High Water'. The last of the flood running up the English Channel sweeps round the east end of the Island, where it meets the water ebbing out of Southampton Water and drives it back in the form of a second high tide.

THE NEEDLES 1890 26177

To the south-west of the Island, the unstable undercliff along the coastline has revealed a wealth of fossils, and evidence that dinosaurs lived on Wight in prehistoric times is regularly found along this area, known as the Back of the Wight. Iguanodon and brachiosaurus were among the dinosaurs that lived in a landscape where massive conifers towered above giant cacti, palms, cycads and other plant life. The fossilized remains of that primeval forest can be seen at low tide in the form of the 'Pine Raft' at the foot of Hanover Point, just off the A3055 near Brook, not far from where the naturally preserved footprints of a three-toed dinosaur can be seen exposed in the clay of Brook Bay.

Some 5,000 years ago Neolithic settlers became the first Islanders to live in one place and farm the land, rather than being nomadic hunter gatherers. It was these people who erected the Island's one surviving man-made Neolithic monument, later known as the Long Stone, on the high ground above Mottistone in the south-west (photograph M399703, opposite). Many centuries later the Anglo-Saxon settlers who came to the Island used it as the place where their elders called men to assembly. It was their Moot (Meeting) Stone, the origin of the name of the nearby hamlet and manor house of Mottistone.

The Bronze Age people who lived on Wight following the Neolithic period buried their dead with pottery and metal artefacts in the ancient burial mounds, known as 'barrows', found on the high downlands across the central belt of the Island. In the 1730s a spectacular collection of Bronze Age finds was unearthed from a burial mound at Arreton Down in the east of the Island. The spearheads, flanged axes, daggers and other metal implements of the Arreton Down Hoard are now in the British Museum in London.

The Bronze Age was followed by the Iron Age, which lasted up to the time of the Roman Conquest of Britain in AD43, when the Isle of Wight became part of the Roman Empire after being 'taken' by the 2nd Legion under the command of the future Emperor, Vespasian. Only one classic hilltop Iron Age fort has been positively identified on Wight, at Chillerton Down, close to the centre of the Island, which is a single-rampart earthwork, complete with ditch. The Romans built no towns or roads on the Island, but left behind fine examples of the villas in which some wealthy Roman Islanders lived. The remains of two – at Morton, (near Brading) and Newport – are open to the public. The Morton villa's remains, including the bath block, central hearing system, frescoes depicting mythical scenes and the magnificent floor mosaics in the preserved west wing, were discovered in 1879. The Roman villa at Cypress Road in Newport was discovered in 1926, when building work revealed extensive remains of a Romano-British farmhouse dating from around AD280.

MOTTISTONE
THE LONG STONE
2005 M399703

The Roman historian Suetonius referred to the Island as 'insula Vecta' in his account of the capture of Wight in AD43. From this derived the name 'Vectis', by which the Island was known through nearly 400 years of Roman rule over Britain. This Roman name for Wight is still widely recalled in the titles of local businesses, notably Southern Vectis, the Island's bus company. Inhabitants of the Island are also sometimes referred to as 'Vectensians'.

Theories abound about the origin of the word 'Wight' in the Island's modern name. Some think it derives from the pre-Roman name of 'Ynys yr Wyth', a Celtic term for 'The island of the Channel', but others believe it comes from the name of Wihtgar, a Saxon chieftain who ruled the Island in the 6th century, the period known as the Dark Ages following the end of Roman rule, when Germanic tribes of Angles, Saxons and Jutes swept into Britain to settle and colonise the land. Wihtgar also gave his name to Carisbrooke (via 'With-gara-burh'), which was the place of his death in AD544.

SANDOWN, THE BEACH 1918 68285

Throughout the Dark Ages and Anglo-Saxon period, the Isle of Wight was regularly attacked by bands of Jutes, Saxons and Vikings hungry for spoils of war and land. However, after the Norman Conquest of England in 1066 and the arrival of a Norman warlord to rule Wight, the Island was never again successfully invaded by foreign armies.

The Isle of Wight was ruled as a semi-independent feudal Norman fiefdom for centuries following the Norman Conquest in 1066, when it was given by William the Conqueror to his kinsman William FitzOsbern. Allegiance on Wight was sworn to FitzOsbern as 'Lord of the Island' rather than the king, a role subsequently granted to the de Redvers family by Henry I after his succession in 1100. Ruling affairs from Carisbrooke Castle, the de Redvers family and their descendants held the Lordship of the Island for virtually 200 years, enjoying near absolute powers, until the end of the 13th century when the Isle of Wight's long period of semi-independence under private ownership was ended.

The final private owner of Wight and independent holder of the Lordship of the Island was actually a lady, Countess Isabella de Fortibus, the last of the ruling dynasty begun by the first Richard de Redvers, who was just 25 when the death of her brother propelled her to unexpected power as the Lady of the Wight. She ruled the Island with a considerable degree of toughness for the next 30 years, but her children all predeceased her, leaving her without direct heirs. On her deathbed in 1293 Isabella was persuaded by King Edward I's officials to sign over the Island to the English Crown, in whose hands it has remained ever since, as fully part of England.

Following this, Wight continued to be controlled by a Lord of the Island, but now someone appointed by the Crown. The title was later restyled as Captain and, finally, Governor. The last Governor was David Seeley, 4th Baron Mottistone, who served from 1992 to 1995 whilst also holding the crown representative title of Lord-Lieutenant. Since 1995 there has been no Governor appointed, and the correct crown representative title for the Isle of Wight now is solely the Lord-Lieutenant.

CARISBROOKE, THE CASTLE GATEWAY c1883 16256

'He who holds Carisbrooke holds the Isle of Wight' ran the traditional maxim. The castle dates back to Norman times, but no domestic buildings of the Norman fortress survive. The most impressive feature of the castle is the 14th-century gatehouse. In 1377 French raiders landed on Wight, attacked and burnt several towns and laid siege to the castle. Peter de Heynoe, Lord of Stenbury, ended the siege by killing the French commander with his crossbow; the arrow slit from which he took aim, 'Heynoe's Loope', is still visible on the west wall. In the 16th century the Italian fortifications engineer Federigo Gianibelli was commissioned to improve Carisbrooke's defences; his curtain walls and bastions are still in very good condition.

King Charles I was imprisoned at Carisbrooke Castle in 1647-48 during the Civil War. He famously became stuck in a window whilst trying to escape, one of several attempts he made to flee the castle. In September 1648 King Charles met with Parliament's Commissioners in Newport in an attempt to reach a settlement, but the treaty negotiations ended in failure and led to the king's eventual return to London and execution in 1649.

One of the features of Carisbrooke Castle is a deep well with a 16th-century tread-wheel that is turned by donkeys, showing the castle's visitors how water was drawn up from the well in the past. It is a tradition for the Carisbrooke donkeys to have names beginning with the letter 'J', in memory of King Charles I – during his imprisonment in the castle he smuggled out coded messages and letters to friends, trying to gain support or plotting escape attempts, which he signed with a 'J' to keep his identity secret. Unfortunately for the hapless king, most of his messages were intercepted.

In 1650 King Charles I's youngest daughter, the 14-year-old Princess Elizabeth, followed her father into incarceration at Carisbrooke Castle, together with her young brother Henry, and she died there after contracting pneumonia. She was interred in the original St Thomas's Church at nearby Newport. When the church was replaced by the present building in 1854-55, now Sts Thomas Minster (dedicated to St Thomas the Apostle and St Thomas Becket), Queen Victoria commissioned a magnificent sculptured monument above her re-located tomb.

CARISBROOKE, THE CASTLE, A DONKEY ON THE TREAD WHEEL c1880 C26302

According to the 8th-century monk and historian the Venerable Bede in 'The Ecclesiastical History of the English People', the Isle of Wight was one of the last places in England to be converted to Christianity, following its conquest in AD686 by Caedwalla, the Christian king of the Anglo-Saxon kingdom of Wessex. Horrified to find the Island still pagan, he ordered a number of Island converts to be baptised by the missionary bishop Wilfrid of York and his team at Brading, where tradition asserts the first of the Island's Christian churches was constructed. Brading's church today is mostly Norman, though with some traces of an older building. There are some beautiful epitaphs to be found in the churchyard, including one beginning 'Forgive, blest shade, the tributary tear, That mourns thy exit from a world like this', which was set to music as a funerary hymn by Dr John Wall Callcott in the 19th century. There are also some fine memorials in the church, notably those of the Oglander family. Sir John Oglander who died in 1655 wrote an early history of the Isle of Wight.

There was apparently an early Saxon church at Bonchurch, near Ventnor, but the older of the village's two surviving churches dedicated to St Boniface as seen today has Norman origins – its windows, square bell tower and porch are much later additions, but the nave and chancel of this picturesque church date from the 11th century. Tradition asserts that the church was refounded by monks from Lyre Abbey in Normandy who came to the Isle of Wight to collect the riches granted them by William FitzOsbern, the Norman warlord who was the first Lord of Wight. FitzOsbern had founded Lyre Abbey in 1045, and granted the abbey the proceeds (tithes on agricultural produce and rents) of six of the Island's churches. The monks discovered a Saxon church in a decrepit state and, in gratitude for their safe delivery from the sea voyage, set about rebuilding it. The tradition of the church's founding by the boat party from Normandy persists to this day in the name of their legendary landing place on the coast east of Bonchurch – Monks Bay.

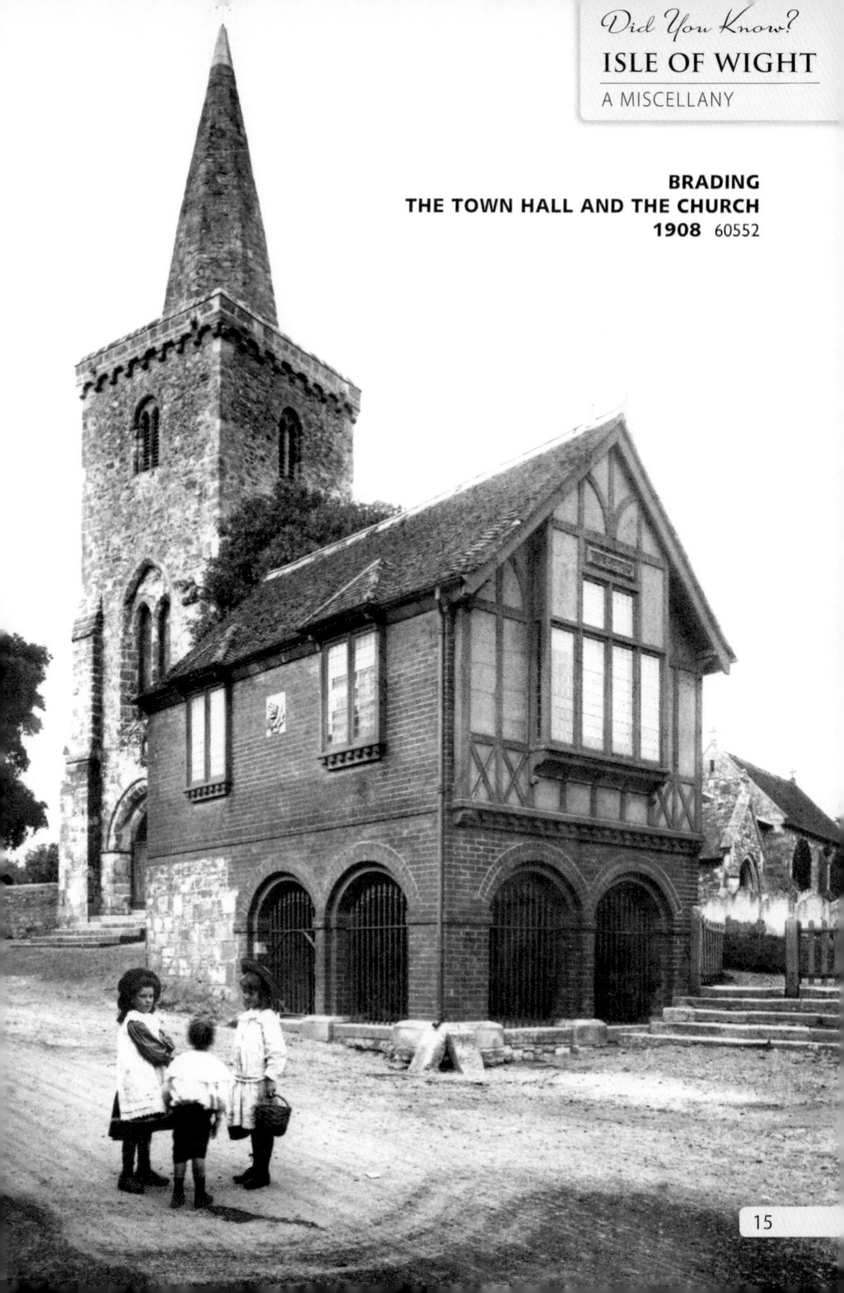

BRADING
THE TOWN HALL AND THE CHURCH
1908 60552

Many fine examples of ecclesiastical Norman architecture on the smaller scale survive on the Isle of Wight. Yaverland Church, probably built c1150 and dedicated to St John the Baptist, is particularly special, with an exceptional chancel arch featuring exquisite carving and deeply cut mouldings on its pillars, and an impressive south door, with a lovely tympanum of diapered pattern and wide mouldings of short pilasters and zigzags, surmounted by a carving of a smiling, friendly face. 21st-century worshippers can still pass through other Norman doorways at Carisbrooke, Wootton and the much-restored church at Northwood, among others.

At Binstead, on the outskirts of Ryde, the Norman entrance arch of the original church now provides access to the churchyard, 'recycled' from the earlier church when the present Church of the Holy Cross was rebuilt in the 19th century. A curious feature of this old Norman arch is an odd little sculpture of a bearded figure of indeterminate gender, known locally as 'The Idol', which, badly weathered, adorns the apex, sitting astride the head of an indeterminate beast, possibly a muzzled bear. The grotesque figure was originally located above the north door of the church and is a 'sheela-na-gig', an Irish term for the enigmatic, quasi-erotic effigies which appear in some old churches. Their true function is unknown, but the theories are that they may have been fertility symbols, protective figures against evil, or a warning against lust. Binstead's churchyard contains several interesting burials, including that of Thomas Sivell, who was mistaken for a smuggler by Portsmouth custom officers and shot dead on board his ship in 1785. His tombstone is carved with an image of a ship at sea, and inscribed with the lines:

All you that pass pray look and see
How soon my life was took from me
By those officers as you hear
They spilled my Blood that was so dear
But God is Good and just and true
And will reward each to their due.

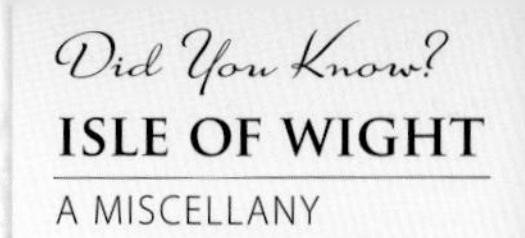

Many people who worshipped in Binstead's church in medieval times would have worked at the important stone quarry on the western fringe of the village at Quarr. The Quarr-Binstead stone was much prized in the past as a hard building material, quarried from pits that can still be traced in woodland alongside today's Quarr footpath. Much of it was shipped across the Solent for use in prestigious building projects on mainland Britain, including the upper section of the White Tower at the Tower of London around 900 years ago, and Winchester Cathedral's magnificent new nave in the 14th century. The quarry also gave its name to the nearby Quarr Abbey, properly the Abbey of Our Lady of the Quarry, the greatest of the medieval religious houses on the Island. Founded as a Cistercian house in 1132, the abbey exercised great power and influence over Island affairs before being dissolved in 1536 by Henry VIII. After spending centuries as farm buildings, the abbey was restored by a group of French Benedictine monks who came to Quarr early in the 20th century, and is still a monastic community of prayer.

QUARR ABBEY c1875 8144

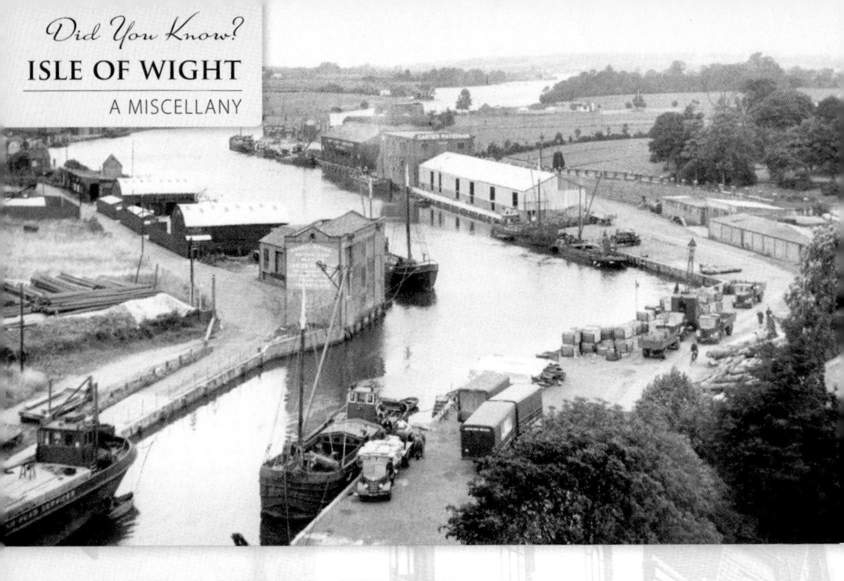

NEWPORT, THE RIVER c1955 N24008

Newport was developed in the late 12th century as the 'new port' for Carisbrooke Castle, from where a trackway ran to the River Medina's navigable limit five miles inland, where vessels could make their way upriver at high tide. The track forked at the west end of the present shopping centre, its 'branch route' running to a ford further up the Medina. Those two tracks are now High Street and Pyle Street ('pyle' means 'ford'). Newport was laid out as a 'new town' on a grid system, with new streets at right angles to High Street and Pyle Street, and others running parallel to the original trackways. In the former category were St James Street, Holyrood Street and Town Lane. The parallel roads to the north of High Street were Lugley Street and Crocker Street.

In the 13th century Countess Isabella de Fortibus, the last private owner of the Island, donated the freehold of virtually all the land on which Newport stood to its townspeople. She kept just a small area at the junction of High Street and Pyle Street, which became known as Castlehold for that reason, and retains the name today.

During the French raid on Wight in 1377 (see page 12), part of the enemy force was ambushed on a track approaching Carisbrooke Castle from Newport, which subsequently became known as Deadman's Lane. Lord Nelson's naval victory at Trafalgar in 1805 led to its re-naming as Trafalgar Road. The bodies of the dead Frenchmen were buried in a mound that became known as 'Noddies Hill'. The name was later corrupted to 'Nodehill', still the name for the area in Newport around Upper St James Street.

In the late 16th century an outbreak of bubonic plague raged through Newport. In St Thomas's Square in Newport stands God's Providence House, traditionally the site of the only house in the town in which no one died during the epidemic, 'by the providence of God', hence the name of the building. In 1701 the house was partly rebuilt following a fire, hence the rebuilding date on a stone panel over the main door, with the inscription 'WIE God's Providence in my inheritance'. It is one of the oldest buildings in Newport, and now houses a tea room and restaurant.

NEWPORT, HOLYROOD STREET 1913 66322

Newport's handsome Guildhall was designed by the famous Regency architect John Nash, who lived at East Cowes, and completed in 1816; the clock tower was a Victorian addition. The Guildhall now houses the Museum of Island History.

Three of Queen Elizabeth I's most influential courtiers hailed from Newport: Dr Edes, her chaplain, Dr James, her doctor, and Thomas Fleming, who became Lord Chief Justice. The witty monarch remarked that one was good for her soul, another for her body, and the third for her goods. Justice Fleming survived into the reign of King James I, when he presided over the trial of Guy Fawkes in January 1606, one of the Gunpowder Plotters who planned to blow up the House of Lords on 5th November 1605 whilst the king was present for the State Opening of Parliament. Inside Newport's Guildhall is a statue of Judge Fleming sitting in a chair carved with a depiction of him presiding at the trial of Guy Fawkes, who was sentenced to death.

NEWPORT, HIGH STREET 1892 30066

YARMOUTH, THE SQUARE c1955 Y4003

West of Newport is the quiet coastal village of Newtown, once an important town and port known as 'Francheville'. A clue to its former importance is its Town Hall, dating from 1699, which now houses a museum. MPs for Newtown returned to Parliament from this humble building included John Churchill, first Duke of Marlborough (1679), and George Canning (1793-96 and 1806-07), who later became Prime Minister.

Yarmouth, the port of the 'West Wight', was granted its first town charter around 1135, officially making it the oldest Island town, but its origins are much earlier. Yarmouth originally developed as a port on the estuary of the Western Yar to replace Thorley, a mile or so inland, which was becoming difficult to reach by ship as the estuary silted up. It first appears in the records in AD991 as 'Ermud'. A strange tale relates how many of Yarmouth's ancient charters were lost. A ship's captain, drunk after a Court Leet dinner in 1784, stole what he thought was a case of wine as he returned to his ship. When he discovered the case was full of books he threw them overboard, consigning many of the town's historical records to the sea.

The Isle of Wight has played an important role in England's history because it controls the approaches to the Solent and the ports of Southampton and Portsmouth. In the 16th century Henry VIII had a number of forts built at each end of the Island to control the approaches across Spithead in the east and The Needles in the west, part of a chain of coastal defences that King Henry established all along the south coast of England. One of the most significant of the Henrician defensive works on the Island was the stone-built square castle at Yarmouth, constructed in 1547 and now in the care of English Heritage.

In 1669 Sir Robert Holmes (c1622-1692) became Governor of the Island, and undertook a general reorganisation of Wight's defences. At Yarmouth he reduced the castle to a more manageable size by demolishing the earthworks, filling in the moat and building a fine house alongside it for himself, now the George Hotel. The old castle entrance was blocked and replaced by the present access on the castle's south side (off Quay Street). The guns were concentrated on the seaward side, backed up by a new battery on the quay. An admiral of Charles II's navy, Sir Robert Holmes is best described as a swashbuckling soldier of fortune with piratical inclinations. The Governorship of the Island gave him access to the lucrative vice-admiralty of the Isle of Wight, Newport and Hampshire, entitling him to two-thirds of the value of all prizes taken in his home waters. Basing his operations from Yarmouth, he made it his mission to prey on foreign ships sailing close to Wight. A good example of his piratical ways is his impressive tomb in the church of St James in Yarmouth. On one of his raids Sir Robert waylaid a ship bound for France that was carrying a headless statue – it was intended to be a portrait of the French king, Louis XI, and the sculptor was accompanying the statue to the French court to complete the head from life. Sir Robert decided the statue would be ideal for his own monument, and had it completed with a sculpture of his own head added to the figure.

The original name for the settlement at what is now Cowes was Shamblord, but this changed after Henry VIII had two block-house forts constructed on either side of the mouth of the River Medina, to protect the entrance to the harbour at Newport. The twin forts became known as the East Cow and the West Cow ('cow' is an old name for a castle, designed to 'cow', or frighten, the enemy). The surviving remnant of the Tudor castle at West Cowes is now the home of the Royal Yacht Squadron, the most famous yacht club in the world, although only the old semi-circular gun platform survives. Nothing at all remains of the Tudor castle at East Cowes.

Land settlement on the east and west banks of the Medina initially concentrated in the 13th century on the east, and East Cowes was once the more important of the two towns. However over the years the development of West Cowes outstripped that of East Cowes, and in 1895 the 'West' prefix was officially dropped – the town on the west bank is Cowes pure and simple now. The town on the east bank remains East Cowes.

COWES, THE ROYAL YACHT SQUADRON
1923 74746x

East Cowes and Cowes are linked together across the River Medina by a chain ferry, known as the Floating Bridge, at the narrow 'Point'. Two heavy chains are fixed on either side of the river, and the machinery on board pulls the ferry across.

The deep, sheltered waters known as Cowes Roads, leading to the small harbour at the mouth of the Medina, were instrumental in the development of Cowes in the 19th century as a yachting mecca and of East Cowes for shipbuilding. Wooden ships were built at Cowes as long ago as the 16th century, thanks to the area's natural advantages of high water and an abundance of raw materials in Parkhurst Forest. Demand for Cowes-built ships grew steadily from Tudor times and from the late 18th century substantial men-o'-war were emerging for the Royal Navy from the East Cowes shipyards. However, many kinds of boats as well as fighting ships were turned out, notably the distinctive Cowes Ketch, which would be mass produced throughout the 19th century and widely employed as a versatile workboat in the Solent and further afield.

COWES, THE FLOATING BRIDGE AND THE DOCKYARD c1960 C173053

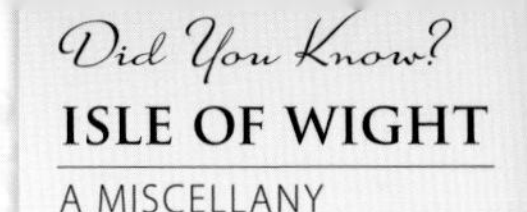

One of the most famous names in the history of Cowes is the shipbuilding firm of J Samuel White & Co Ltd, known locally as 'Sammy White's', which began in Cowes in the early 19th century, when Thomas White acquired the old Nye shipyard on the east bank of the Medina and moved his business there from Kent. The company expanded and became J Samuel White's in 1898, under Thomas's grandson, John Samuel. Under this identity it remained an internationally-respected brand for decades to come. 'White's built – well-built' became an entirely accurate marketing slogan for the company. 'Sammy White's' built over 2,000 vessels at various shipyards at Cowes between 1803 and their closure in 1963, including warships in the Napoleonic Wars, destroyers and submarines for the Royal Navy in the 20th century, and RNLI lifeboats. The firm also built ships for foreign navies, in particular the Polish destroyer 'Blyskawica', which helped to save Cowes when the town was heavily bombed during the Second World War, in May 1942. It was a measure of White's importance that the Germans were trying to put them out of action. The West Cowes part of the dockyard of J S White in the 1950s is seen in photograph C173053 on the opposite page, with a ship being fitted out for the Royal Navy, whilst the shipyard's distinctive 80 ton 'hammerhead' giant cantilever crane looms behind it.

Cowes Maritime Museum in Beckford Road has a collection of some fine model ships built by J Samuel White & Co Ltd. The museum also displays paintings, logbooks, model ships, and yacht designs by Uffa Fox, the master yachtsman and designer who was born at East Cowes in 1898 and lived most of his life on the Island. He conceived, designed and built the airborne lifeboat at Cowes during the Second World War, and without doubt many airmen in the latter part of the war owed their lives to his brilliance and tenacity.

EAST COWES, SAUNDERS-ROE SEAPLANE BASE c1955 E139005

The Island's other industrial giant of the past was also based at East Cowes, Saunders-Roe, an aero- and marine-engineering company, particularly known for making giant flying boats for commercial passenger use. Photograph E139005 (above) was taken in the mid 1950s looking across the Medina from Cowes, on the west bank, to the main Saunders-Roe yards at East Cowes. The view is framed by the wing of a Short Sunderland flying boat that was being used in the development of control systems etc for the SR45 Princess flying boat then under construction in the East Cowes factory. Saunders-Roe also built other vehicles, such as lifeboats, as well as Sir Malcolm Campbell's Blue Bird K3, designed by Fred Cooper of Saunders-Roe, in which Campbell broke the water speed record 3 times, twice in 1937 and again in 1938. After a series of company changes and merges over the years, what used to be Saunders-Roe is now part of GKN Aerospace Services, which continues the tradition of aircraft component design and production at East Cowes.

Another record-breaking vehicle was built on the Isle of Wight, the jet-propelled Thrust 2, which broke the World Land Speed Record in 1983 at 633.468 mph, driven by Richard Noble. It was designed by John Ackroyd and built at the Ranalagh Works in Fishbourne.

The Isle of Wight was at the forefront of hovercraft development. In 1959 the world's first air-riding vehicle was unveiled at East Cowes, the hovercraft SR.N1, invented and designed by Sir Christopher Cockerell and built by Saunders-Roe. The SR.N1 was followed by bigger, better hovercraft turned out by Saunders-Roe both before and after its takeover by Westland Aircraft Ltd and later absorption in the British Hovercraft Corporation in the 1960s. In 1965 the world's first regular hovercraft passenger service was launched by Hovertravel between Ryde and Southsea on the mainland. The Ryde-Southsea hovercraft passenger service is still operational today, taking just ten minutes to cross the Solent.

The Island's other famous post-war industrial product of the 20th century was the Islander light aircraft which first flew in 1965, developed and produced at the Bembridge Airport base of Britten-Norman. The name of this innovative twin-engined utility aircraft with the minimum of complex systems recalls not only its development on Wight but also its unrivalled island-hopping capabilities, able to operate from short, rough airstrips. Over 750 Islander aircraft are still in operation around the world.

RYDE
HOVERTRAVEL'S FREEDOM 90
2005 R76701

In the second half of the 19th century, the Prime Minister Lord Palmerston ordered a ring of forts to be built around Portsmouth to protect the dockyard and anchorage at Spithead against a perceived threat from France. These included four sea forts built on shoals in the Solent: Spitbank Fort (nearest Portsmouth), No Man's Land Fort (nearest Ryde), Horse Sand Fort (roughly in the middle) and St Helens Fort, built to protect the St Helens Road anchorage, very close to the Island's north-east coast. St Helens Fort is now privately owned and not open to the public, but can be visited once a year, usually in August, when a very low tide reveals a causeway from the beach. It is a tradition for a mass procession of local people to walk along the causeway to the fort; they are then careful to beat the tide back to the beach, where a barbeque is held after the excursion.

Also at this time the Isle of Wight's own coastal defences were strengthened. New gun batteries were put up east and west, protecting both approaches to the Solent. The remains of the batteries at The Needles and Puckpool, east of Ryde, are now open to the public. The Needles Old Battery at West High Down, Alum Bay, was built in the 1860s. Two 12-ton guns were hauled up into position, while tunnels through the cliff led to a searchlight station and parade ground. The New Battery at the Needles, slightly further east, followed in the 1890s. Thanks to its underground facilities, the site of the Old Battery was used when Saunders-Roe of Cowes developed a rocket testing programme there between 1956 and 1971, where the Island company could secretly test-fire the engines it had manufactured at East Cowes for the Black Knight and Black Arrow rockets. (The rockets themselves were later put through their paces in Woomera, Australia). Two underground rooms in the New Battery now house an exhibition about those secret tests. Test firing of the rockets on the Needles headland was carried out until the site was abandoned in the 1970s. It is now a ghostly, incongruous promenade to nowhere on the edge of the cliffs. Information boards at the abandoned rocket-test site tell the story.

It was also at the time of the perceived threat from France in the mid 19th century that two massive defensive forts were constructed on the western side of the Island, Fort Victoria near Yarmouth, and Fort Albert at Colwell Bay, constructed on an artificial island at Cliff End to guard the western approach to the Solent, the 'Needles Passage'. Fort Albert is seen on the extreme left of photograph C452004, below. This tower fort housed 29 guns in four tiers, its defences enhanced with batteries on the cliffs above, but it soon became obsolete in its original function, with the development of armoured ships. It took on a new role in 1886 when it became a launching station for the Brennan torpedo to protect the Needles Passage, but this too had become obsolete by 1906. Fort Albert was used as an observation tower during the Second World War but its military function ceased in 1957 and, now in private ownership, it has been converted into residential flats. All that remains of Fort Albert's 'sister fort', Fort Victoria west of Yarmouth, is its sea-facing casemates (fortified gun emplacements), forming the centrepiece of the Victoria Country Park.

Other Victorian defensive works on the west of the Island included the Warden Point battery overlooking Totland Bay, Fort Redoubt, built to prevent the French landing at Freshwater Bay, and the military road, the stretch of what is now the A3055 along the south-west coast of the Island (now in danger of eroding into the sea) from Niton to Freshwater Bay, built in 1860 to supply the coastal garrisons. Victorian forts and batteries were also constructed on the east coast, at Bembridge, Nodes Point, Redcliff, Puckpool, Sandown, Steynewood, and Yaverland.

COLWELL BAY, FORT ALBERT c1955 C452004

OSBORNE HOUSE, FROM THE NORTH-EAST c1883 16267

In 1845, five years after their marriage, Queen Victoria and her husband Prince Albert adopted the Isle of Wight as their holiday home, where they could enjoy some privacy away from the ceremonial courts. The royal couple bought the Osborne House estate, near East Cowes, demolished the original house and built a magnificent Italianate mansion which Prince Albert designed himself, with the assistance of Thomas Cubitt, the renowned London builder. The mansion was surrounded by large gardens with rare trees, and Queen Victoria had a Swiss chalet erected in the grounds for the royal children to play in. Her daughters used its kitchen to serve tea to their maids.

After the death of Prince Albert in 1861 Queen Victoria went into deep mourning and retreated to the Isle of Wight to live in seclusion at Osborne for a considerable time. According to some sources, it was there that the Victoria Sandwich sponge cake was 'invented' by the queen's chefs, in an attempt to cheer her up and encourage her to socialise more by holding tea parties.

In 1876 Queen Victoria became Empress of India. Although she never visited India she became fascinated by all things Indian, and had the Durbar Room constructed at Osborne, in Indian style, between 1890-91 to provide a state banqueting room. The name 'Durbar' derives from an Indian word meaning both a state reception and a hall for gatherings. The room was designed by Lockwood Kipling, father of the writer Rudyard Kipling, and the principal craftsman was Bhai Ram Singh. The Indian architecture and rich embellishment of every surface from floor to ceiling transports the visitor to the world of India, and the room exhibits the exquisite gifts given to Queen Victoria by the Indian people. The Indian symbolism of the decorations includes Ganesh, the elephant god of good fortune, and the spectacular peacock over the chimney-piece.

Queen Victoria used Osborne as her favourite winter retreat for the rest of her life, and died there on 22nd January 1901. Osborne House has been in the care of English Heritage since 1984. In 2001, the centenary year of Queen Victoria's death, the dining room of the house was refurbished and shows the table in the process of being laid for dinner.

OSBORNE HOUSE, THE STATE APARTMENTS THE INDIAN DURBAR ROOM 1908 60585

RYDE, THE PIER 1897 40353

Ryde is the nearest Island port to the mainland. Victorian passengers arriving by paddle-steamer would disembark at Ryde Pier, which originally opened in 1814, sufficiently long at 530 metres (1,740 feet) to allow ferries to berth even at low tide, when the sea retreats half a mile from the shore. Since then the pier has been twice extended to its present 681 metres (2,234 feet), making Ryde Pier the second-longest seaside pier in England, eclipsed only by the pier at Southend-on-Sea in Essex. Ryde Pier is actually three separate piers in one: the original pedestrian pier, the now-disused tramway pier alongside it, and the railway pier between Pier Head and Esplanade stations, opened in 1880. Passengers can still travel by rail from the pierhead at Ryde through to Shanklin, on old electric stock that used to run on the London Underground.

The 1970s' classic BBC TV sit-com 'Some Mothers Do 'Ave Em', starring Michael Crawford as the accident-prone Frank Spencer, was created and written by an Isle of Wight man, Raymond Allen, from Ryde. The town's street names feature in several episodes of the popular series.

Ryde takes its name from the old English word 'rith' (pronounced 'rithe'), meaning a small stream. That stream is today's Monktonmead brook, which runs through the town (though now largely buried beneath it) to the sea. Ryde began as two small hamlets, Lower Ryde, a cluster of fishermen's cottages at the water's edge, and Upper Ryde, focussed on St Thomas's Chapel, built in 1719 to save local people a six-mile trek to the then parish church at Newchurch. In 1780 the two hamlets were linked by the construction of the appropriately-named Union Street. The building of its pier in 1814 turned Ryde into the Island's main passenger port, and soon the town had developed into a very fashionable 'watering place'. Some street names in Ryde recall members of England's most aristocratic families who had holiday villas there in the early 19th century, such as Buckingham Road and Buckingham Close (named after the first Duke of Buckingham, whose holiday home is now called Buckingham Villas, converted into flats) and Spencer Road, named after the 2nd Earl Spencer, whose holiday home was what is now Westfield Park House.

RYDE, UNION STREET 1905 53165

VENTNOR, FROM THE PIER 1918 68273

Ventnor transformed itself from an obscure fishing hamlet to a fashionable holiday resort during the last half of the 19th century. However, the south-facing town lies at the foot of a steep hill, and the development of the town between the hill and the English Channel was, of necessity, strung out along a series of terraces, unique on the Island, connected by climbing roads of Alpine proportions. This sheltered location of Ventnor, protected from harsher northern influences by the highest hills on the Isle of Wight, has given the area a famously mild climate that aids the growth of luxuriant vegetation in the town's steep gardens. In 1830 the eminent physician Sir James Clark made the resort's reputation by comparing its equitable climate to that of Madeira, and Victorian Ventnor became a refuge for consumptives. In a few short years four large homes for sufferers from tuberculosis were established in the resort, where the good weather, fresh air and regime of long bracing walks did a great deal to alleviate their condition.

Given the accepted status of the town as a health resort, Ventnor was an obvious place for the construction of the Royal National Hospital for Diseases of the Chest, also known as the Royal National Hospital for Consumptive Diseases, which opened in 1869, three years after the arrival of the railway – patients travelled to Ventnor on the 'Invalids' Express'. The hospital was famous for the success of its treatments and lasted for the best part of a century, until made redundant by modern medicine. Little remains of its once extensive buildings, and its grounds where medicinal plants once grew are now Ventnor's Botanic Garden. However, one part of the Botanic Garden has been preserved just as it was at the time the hospital was there, the Palm Garden. The palm trees were donated by Queen Victoria, who was a patron of the hospital and visited several times, and were planted where she recommended they should go.

The Isle of Wight has long been known as the 'Garden Isle' where plants flourish because of the mild climate, and a number of unusual, historically important or exotic plants and trees from foreign lands can be found in its gardens or plant collections; these include the Chinese Fan Palm in Ventnor Botanic Garden, one of the first to be introduced into Britain, and the splendid Cork Oaks at Osborne House. Many rare or unusual native plants also flourish in the diverse landscape of the Island – nowhere else in Britain has such a spectacular range of habitats within such a small geographical area. The wood calamint (Calamintha sylvatica) is found only on the Island, growing on shady chalk banks from the west of Newport to Yarmouth. Other rare native plant species found on Wight include the little-known Field Cow-wheat (Melampyrum arvense), the Autumn Squill (Scilla autumnalis) and the Pyramidal Orchid (Anacamptis pyramidalis), voted the County Flower of the Isle of Wight in 2002 in a poll by the wild flora conservation charity Plantlife. More information about both native and exotic rare plants and trees on the Island can be found in the excellent Rare Plant Trail produced by the Wightlink ferry company – download it from:
www.wightlink.co.uk/isle-of-wight-guide-and-events/walking/the-rare-plant-trail

Bonchurch, east of Ventnor, stands on the steep slopes of St Boniface Down. Both the hillside and village are named after St Boniface, who took Christianity to Germany and was martyred there in AD755. There are two churches in the village, both of which are dedicated to St Boniface. The 'old church' dates from at least the 11th century (see page 14). The 'new' St Boniface Church dates from the 1840s. In its churchyard is the grave of the controversial poet and intellectual rebel Algernon Charles Swinburne (1837-1909), who spent his childhood at his family home of East Dene, near Bonchurch. Swinburne's grave was the subject of the poem 'A Singer Asleep' by the novelist and poet Thomas Hardy, who wrote the work whilst sitting beside it. Bonchurch became a fashionable holiday centre for writers and artists in the 19th century, who stayed in large villas that they rented for the season; these included Charles Dickens, who wrote part of 'David Copperfield' while staying at 'Winterbourne' in Bonchurch in 1849. The house is now a hotel where visitors can stay in the David Copperfield Room.

BONCHURCH, THE VILLAGE 1890 26151x

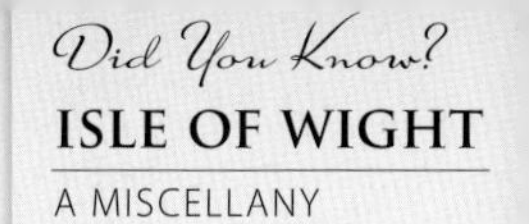

A few miles north-west from Ventnor is the pretty village of Godshill (see photograph on title page). Its parish church of All Saints is the largest medieval church on the island. It has fine examples of 14th-century 'decorated style' windows, and the tower and transept arches are of the same period. The roof is black oak with over a mile of timbers. The church is popularly known as 'the Church of the Lily Cross' because of the large 15th- or 16th-century wall painting on the east wall of the south transept of a 'lily crucifix', depicting Christ crucified on a triple-branched flowering lily. A 'lily crucifix' or 'lily cross' is a very rare medieval Christian symbol, linking the crucifixion of Jesus with the lily as a symbol of the purity and sinlessness of His mother, the Virgin Mary. The 'Lily Cross' in the church at Godshill was covered over with whitewash during the changes in religious attitudes of the 16th-century Reformation and rediscovered in the 19th century. This artwork is unique in the British Isles – the only other examples of the Lily Cross theme in Britain are found in stained-glass windows in a few churches around the country.

There is another important medieval wall painting in Shorwell's medieval church of St Peter, west of Godshill. This rare work over the north door of the church depicts scenes from the life of St Christopher, and dates from the mid 15th century. Amongst many other items of interest in this fascinating church are two carved stone corbels supporting the main roof beam – one represents sins, and the other represents death. There is a fine memorial in the church to Sir John Leigh, who died in 1629. His nine-month-old grandson died before Sir John could be buried. They now share a tomb and epitaph: *'Inmate in grave, he took his grandchild heir, Whose soul did haste to make to him repair, And so to heaven along as little page, With him did post, to wait upon his age'.*

West of Ventnor, and overlooking the English Channel from high on the Island's south downs above St Catherine's Point, near Niton, is Britain's only surviving medieval lighthouse, known locally as The Pepper Pot. The 14th-century lighthouse took its official name of St Catherine's Oratory from a now-lost small oratory that was attached to it, where the monk who tended the light said prayers for stricken mariners. The old medieval lighthouse is now an ancient monument, and its function is fulfilled nowadays by the 19th-century lighthouse with its distinctive octagonal tower that stands on St Catherine's Point. St Catherine's Lighthouse is regularly open for visitor tours during the year – check the Trinity House website for opening times: www.trinityhouse.co.uk. On 1st June 1943, during the Second World War, a bomb landed directly on the engine house of St Catherine's lighthouse station, killing the three keepers on duty who had taken shelter there. Their last log can be seen in the log book on show for visitors touring the lighthouse, and a Union Jack flag is displayed on a wall as a mark of respect to them.

NITON, ST CATHERINE'S LIGHTHOUSE 1903 50699

BLACKGANG CHINE, THE UPPER CHINE c1883 16444

West of St Catherine's Point is Blackgang Chine, one of the Island's oldest and biggest visitor attractions, now in the form of an amusement park around themes such as smugglers and pirates. The business began in 1843, when Alexander Dabell opened a shop at the entrance to the great cleft in the yellow sandstone and blue clays of the cliff that plunged to the seashore, and visitors flocked to enjoy its spectacular paths, dramatic waterfall and colourful scenery. The following year Mr Dabell added to its attractions when he acquired the body of a dead whale found floating in the Solent. He sold the blubber, had the bones bleached and put the skeleton on display in a tin shed at the top of the chine. The whale skeleton still survives, now housed in a modern building. Victorian visitors could sit on a 'wishing chair' inside the huge tunnel formed by the whale's ribs, and make a wish inside the belly of a whale. Photograph 16444 (above) shows Blackgang Chine as it was in the 1880s. Since then, all this cliff face has fallen into the sea, and the very top of the gorge path is all that remains of the original spectacular Blackgang Chine.

Many of the Island's coastal resorts were equipped with seaside piers in the 19th century. Sadly, the piers at Cowes (photograph 50797B on page 47), Seaview (a graceful chain-suspension pier out to the steamer landing stage), Shanklin and Ventnor have all been lost. Shanklin's was destroyed by hurricane-force winds during the 'Great Storm' of October 1987, and Sandown's pier, built in 1879, is now the only surviving Victorian pier on the Island's east coast.

Sandown's 'village by the sandy shore' became the home at the end of the 18th century of John Wilkes (1725-1797), the radical journalist, political agitator and former Mayor of London, when he moved into Sandham Cottage at Sandham, slightly inland from Sandown Bay (now part of Sandown). Wilkes referred to his cottage as his 'Villakin' and occupied it from 1788 to 1797. No doubt he preferred it to the Tower of London, where he had briefly been imprisoned in1763 for criticising King George III in a pamphlet. His cottage no longer stands, but its site is commemorated with a plaque in Wilkes Road in Sandown, on the wall of the shop building at the corner of Wilkes Road and 43-45 High Street.

SEAVIEW
THE SUSPENSION PIER
1913 66340x

SANDOWN, THE ESPLANADE 1895 36249

The presence of John Wilkes at Sandown was a major influence in establishing the resort as a fashionable holiday location among the London gentry in the late 18th century. Many of those visitors came to see Wilkes at his 'Villakin', and he enjoyed being hospitable – as John Bullar recorded in his 'Historical and Picturesque Guide to the Isle of Wight' (1810), Sandown Cottage became 'one of those fancy places which the summer visitants to the Isle of Wight seldom omitted in their excursions; a circumstance highly acceptable to its master who refused admission to no-one'.

Sandown and its twin resort of Shanklin, a couple of miles to the south, are connected by a long promenade that winds around the curve of Shanklin Bay. Nowadays this part of the coast offers some of the safest bathing on the Island, but in prehistoric times it was roamed by dinosaurs. At extreme low tide, dinosaur footprints and fossilized bones can be seen in the exposed rocks in the northern part of Sandown Bay. The Dinosaur Isle Museum at Sandown has on display the fossilized remains of a species of small dinosaur found at Yaverland which is the only known specimen in the world; appropriately, it has been named 'Yaverlandia'.

The original settlement of Shanklin is the area known as the Old Village, which developed around the head of Shanklin Chine, a fissure in the cliffs with a spectacular ravine and pretty waterfall. This natural feature was one of the Island's earliest tourist haunts. In the summer of 1819 the Romantic poet John Keats was staying in the Old Village for the good of his health, and wrote that he wished he had a penny for every visitor passing his lodgings en route to the chine. Keats lodged at Eglantine Cottage, which now comprises the rear part of Keats Cottage, at the top of the Old Village at 76 High Street. His visit lasted for two months, and he worked on some of his best-known works whilst he was there – 'Hyperion', 'Lamia' and 'Otho the Great'. His stay in Shanklin is commemorated in the name of Keats Green, a cliff-top walk above the seafront of the newer Shanklin that developed as a holiday resort in the 19th century.

SHANKLIN, IN THE OLD VILLAGE 1913 66210x

SHANKLIN, FROM THE PIER 1913 66194

Shanklin may have lost its seaside pier but it still has the modern incarnation of another attraction for its Victorian visitors, the hydraulic cliff lift erected in the 1890s to allow easy access between the seafront and the town on the steep cliff above the beach. In those days the fare for the lift was 1 penny to go down and 2 pennies to go up. Photograph 66194 (above) shows the original cliff lift, which was demolished in the 1950s and replaced with the more modernistic, fully enclosed lift that now graces the seafront.

Towards the end of the Second World War, Operation PLUTO ('Pipe-Line Under the Ocean') operated initially from the Island, a project devised to fuel the Allied advance from Normandy after D-Day in 1944. Feeder pipes brought petrol and aviation spirit from the mainland to pumping stations at Sandown and Shanklin, and the first PLUTO lines were laid from Shanklin Pier to Cherbourg in France. An exhibition of PLUTO memorabilia can be seen at Shanklin Chine, as well as a short section of the piping alongside a path.

North of Sandown is Brading, which acquired its town charter in 1280 from King Edward I and thus has unique status as the only Island town to receive its first charter from the reigning monarch rather than the Lord of Island; this led to it being known as 'The King's Town'. Brading retains much of its former municipal 'furniture', such as its stocks and whipping post which are preserved in the Old Town Hall near the church (seen in photograph 60552 on page 15), which also features a tiny lock-up.

The name of the Bull Ring in the centre of Brading is a legacy of the bull-baiting that used to take place here, attended by the Mayor in full regalia. The Governor of the Island donated money to purchase the bull, which was then tethered and attacked by a dog, known as the Mayor's Dog. Afterwards, the meat of the bull was donated to the poor of the town. All that remains of this tradition now is the bull's iron tethering ring, which has been moved from the centre of the Bull Ring and set into the ground outside the New Town Hall, adjacent to a large wooden carving of a bull by local artist Paul Sivell.

A famous Island dwelling is Little Jane's Cottage at Brading, up the B39 bridle path from The Mall, which was the home of young Jane Squibb in the late 18th century. In 1797 Legh Richmond came to the parish of Brading and Yaverland as its curate and set up a Bible class for local children, one of whom was Jane. Her piety and enthusiasm for learning made a great impression on him, but sadly she was of delicate constitution and died aged 15. In later years Legh Richmond wrote some inspirational moral tales, 'The Annals of the Poor', which enjoyed a large readership. He incorporated tales of several real-life residents of Brading in his tales, one of whom was 'Jane the Young Cottager'.

During his time as curate-in-charge of Brading and Yaverland, Reverend Legh Richmond also invented the boards that are now widely used in churches all over the world to display the hymn numbers being used for church services.

BRADING, THE STOCKS 1908 60555

Reverend Richmond also immortalised Elizabeth Wallbridge of Arreton in his book 'The Dairyman's Daughter', a widely read Christian tract of the 19th century. A young woman whose life was transformed after hearing a sermon, she became very devout and devoted much time to studying the Bible, especially when her health failed. Reverend Richmond often visited and talked with her, and those discussions inspired his book. Elizabeth died in 1801 and was laid to rest Arreton churchyard, where her gravestone is notable for its long inscription and became a place of pilgrimage for Victorian tourists.

Bembridge is the most easterly settlement on the Island. Bembridge Mill, built around 1700, is Wight's last surviving windmill, seen in photograph B64301 on page 49. Also known as Knowle Mill, this Grade 1 listed building is a four-storey tower windmill with four common, cloth spread sails. It was winded by hand by means of an endless chain which hung from a chainwheel at the rear of the boat-shaped cap down to the ground. It was in continuous use until 1913, producing flour, meal, and cattle feed with two pairs of underdriven millstones. It is now cared for by the National Trust and open to visitors.

SPORTING ISLE OF WIGHT

Probably the most famous yacht club in the world is The Royal Yacht Squadron at Cowes, based in the former Tudor stronghold of West Cowes Castle. Originally founded in London in 1815 with 42 upper-crust members, it became the Royal Yacht Club in 1820 on the accession of George IV, a notable member. In 1825 the club began a long association with the Isle of Wight when it moved to the Island and first set up home at Cowes, and in 1833 the club restyled itself the Royal Yacht Squadron – so called because in those days, boats were armed. The Royal Yacht Squadron serves as the focal point for Cowes Week, the world's biggest and most prestigious international yachting regatta and easily the most well-known event on the Isle of Wight's social and sporting calendar. Cowes Week takes place every August, staging around 40 races each day in which over 1,000 boats compete. The Regatta in 1903 is seen in full swing in photograph 50797B (opposite), which also shows the now-lost Victoria Pier of Cowes in the foreground.

Another sailing club based in Cowes is the Island Sailing Club, which organises the Round the Island yacht race every summer, a gruelling 50 mile anti-clockwise race around the Isle of Wight that is one of the largest yacht races in the world, with around 1800 vessels competing. It is a spectacular sight to see all the yachts taking part, with the skyline filled with colourful sails. The first international yacht race around the Island took place in 1851, when the New York Yacht Club challenged the Royal Yacht Squadron to a race as part of the celebrations of the Great Exhibition in London. The schooner 'America' was sent across the Atlantic, and proceeded to beat all the English yachts in a race that lasted more than ten hours. Having been donated by the Royal Yacht Squadron, the winner's trophy was subsequently named the 'America's Cup' after the boat. That cup is now the oldest sporting trophy in the world, and is awarded to the winner of what is now the prestigious America's Cup yacht race.

COWES, THE REGATTA 1903 50797B

Members of the Island Sailing Club also take part in a very unusual cricket match each year, which is one of Britain's strangest sporting events – the Brambles Cricket Match, played on the Brambles sandbank in the Solent against members of the Royal Southern Yacht Club at Hamble, in Hampshire. Just once each year, for about one hour, the Brambles sandbank appears in the Solent, about halfway between Southampton and the Isle of Wight. The two teams head out to the sandbank, many dressed appropriately in cricket whites, and play a quick game of cricket before the sea reclaims the pitch. Both teams then adjourn to the Isle of Wight for a celebratory dinner.

For those who prefer their racing to be on dry land, the Isle of Wight Marathon is the oldest continuously held marathon in the United Kingdom, having been run every year since 1957, making it also one of the earliest to be held in this country. Held every October, the race starts and finishes in Ryde.

QUIZ QUESTIONS

Answers on page 52.

1. Has the Isle of Wight ever had its own king?
2. Which pop star from the Isle of Wight was known as 'The Singing Milkman', and why?
3. The Isle of Wight is mentioned in which popular Beatles song?
4. Something rare called a Glanville Fritillary is found on the Isle of Wight – what is it?
5. What is the highest point on the Isle of Wight, and why is it known as a 'Marilyn'?
6. When and why was the Isle of Wight bombed with beetles? Yes, beetles!
7. Which Isle of Wight company has the longest company name in the UK?
8. The Island currently organises the largest festival in Britain of which activity?
9. What sport is played by the Wightlink Raiders?
10. Marketing the 'different-ness' of the Island became something of an art form in the mid 20th century. The most enduring example was the production of postcards featuring views of the 'Six Wonders of Wight' – can you list them?

BEMBRIDGE, THE OLD WINDMILL c1955 B64301

RECIPE

ROASTED GARLIC SAUCE

The Isle of Wight has become famous for the garlic grown at The Garlic Farm at Mersley Farm, near Newchurch, the UK's largest specialist garlic grower. The Garlic Farm produces a wide range of garlic and garlic products, which can be bought online from the farm's website, www.thegarlicfarm.co.uk, which also tells the fascinating story of how garlic came to be grown commercially on the Island, originally as a way of making local food more palatable for the crew members of a squadron of Free French torpedo boats who were stationed on the Island during the Second World War. The Garlic Farm also holds an annual Garlic Festival each August, which is one of the Island's biggest events and one of the UK's top food festivals – see www.garlic-festival.co.uk for details.

This quick and easy recipe makes a lovely garlicky dressing for salads or pasta, or to use as a sauce for grilled chicken breasts, steaks or fish. If you want to make this thicker, to use as a tangy dip, just leave out the water.

6 garlic cloves, in their skins
3 tablespoonfuls mayonnaise
170g/6oz carton thick natural Greek-style yogurt (or three tablespoonfuls)
2 tablespoonfuls of water
Salt and freshly ground black pepper

Pre-heat the oven to 220°C/425°F/Gas Mark 7.

Place the garlic cloves on a baking tray and roast them in the pre-heated oven for 15 minutes. Set them aside to cool for a few minutes. When they are cool enough to handle, peel off the skin and place the cooked garlic flesh in a food processor or blender. Add the remaining ingredients and process it all together until it is smooth. Chill in the fridge until required.

RECIPE

LAVENDER SCONES

Another unusual crop grown on the Island is lavender, at the Isle of Wight Lavender Farm at Staplehurst Grange, Staplers Road, near Newport (www.lavender.co.uk), where in spring and summer the fields are purple with fragrant flowers. Lavender is used in a wide variety of products, but can also be used in cooking – the tearoom at the lavender farm is famous for its lavender ice-cream. Dried lavender flowers give these scones a lovely fragrant flavour. Use a variety of 'sweet' English lavender rather than the tufted French lavender variety ('Lavandula stoechas'), which has an unpleasant flavour and can be toxic. English lavender varieties 'Lavandula angustifolia' (sometimes called 'Lavandula officinalis') and 'Lavandula Munstead' give the best results for culinary purposes. Choose lavender sprigs that are deep purple and still in bud, before the flowers have opened. This amount makes 8-9 scones.

225g/8oz plain flour
1 teaspoonful bicarbonate of soda
2 teaspoonfuls cream of tartar
50g/2oz softened butter
25g/1oz caster sugar
2 teaspoonfuls fresh, or 1 teaspoonful dried, lavender florets
150ml/ ¼ pint semi-skimmed milk, warmed slightly

Pre-heat the oven to 200°C/400°F/Gas Mark 6, and grease a baking tray. Sieve the flour, bicarbonate of soda and cream of tartar into a mixing bowl. Rub in the butter, then stir in the sugar and lavender. Stir in the milk, using a round-bladed knife, to form a soft dough. Knead the dough gently for a few seconds, then lightly roll or pat it out on a floured surface to about 2cms (¾ inch) thick. Use a fluted cutter about 6cms (2½ inches) in diameter to stamp out scone rounds, then re-roll the trimmings and cut out more. Place the rounds on the baking tray and bake in the pre-heated oven for 8-10 minutes, until they are well-risen and golden brown – do not overcook them, or their soft, light texture will be spoiled. Cool on a wire tray. These are lovely eaten whilst they are still warm, spread with butter, jam and clotted or very thick cream.

QUIZ ANSWERS

1. Yes, once! The Isle of Wight had its own monarch in 1444 when Henry Beauchamp, Duke of Warwick, was crowned 'King of the Wight' by Henry VI of England, who is believed to have honoured the Duke of Warwick in this way simply so his friend would be nearer himself in rank. Warwick's short 'reign' of about two years ended with his death in 1446 at the age of 22, leaving no male heir, and the regal title expired.
2. 'The Singing Milkman' was Craig Douglas (real name Terence Perkins), born in 1941 at Newport on the Isle of Wight. He was employed as a local milkman before becoming a professional singer, hence his nickname. He was a popular star of the 1950s and 60s and had nine UK Top 40 singles, but is best known for his 1959 chart topper, 'Only Sixteen'.
3. 'When I'm 64', from the Beatles' 1967 album 'Sergeant Pepper's Lonely Hearts Club Band', which features the line 'Every summer we can rent a cottage on the Isle of Wight, if it's not too dear'.
4. A Glanville Fritillary is a very rare butterfly named after Lady Eleanor Glanville, the first person to catch and catalogue specimens of it in the 1690s. The Glanville Fritillary is now a vulnerable species in Britain and virtually restricted to coastal landslips on the southern half of the Isle of Wight. The Island is also an important stronghold of the Red Squirrel, which is under threat on mainland Britain.
5. The highest point on the Island is at St Boniface Down overlooking Ventnor. It is 241 metres (791 feet) above sea level, which makes it a 'Marilyn', the name for a mountain or hill in England more than 150 metres (492 ft) high. The term derives from the name Marilyn Monroe, as a playful connection with the term 'Munro' that is used to define a mountain in Scotland with a height of more than 914.4 metres (3,000 feet).

6. During the Second World War, Colorado beetles were dropped by the German Luftwaffe on the Isle of Wight in 1943, not far from Chale village, in the south of the Island. This was the first recorded drop in Germany's 'beetle bomb' offensive against the vital British potato crop (the Colorado beetle is a major pest of potatoes). The Germans were obviously aware of the Island's wartime status among the nation's top potato-growing counties – but they were over precise in the delivery. The cardboard boxes used were each filled with exactly 100 or 50 beetles, so the young evacuees employed to round them up knew precisely how many they had to catch! The children were sworn to secrecy to avoid the risk of panic and the 'beetle bomb' episode remained 'hush hush' until 1970.

7. The Red Funnel ferry company began when The Isle of Wight Royal Mail Steam Packet Company began regular services between Cowes and Southampton in 1820. 41 years later that company merged with a rival to form 'The Southampton, Isle of Wight and South of England Royal Mail Steam Packet Company Limited', which is still its 'official' name and the longest company title in England – no wonder it is known as Red Funnel for short!

8. The Isle of Wight Walking Festival is held over two weeks every May and is the biggest event of its kind in the country. Thousands of people enjoy over 250 graded and accompanied walks, ranging from short walks for children to a marathon 24-hour walk all round the Island, following its coastal path.

9. The Wightlink Raiders play ice hockey in the English National Ice Hockey League, playing out of the Ryde Arena. The Raiders were the English National League South Division One Champions in the 2010-11 season.

10. The 'Six Wonders of the Isle of Wight' are: Ryde where you walk; Cowes you cannot milk; Newport you cannot bottle; Lake where there is no water; Freshwater you cannot drink; and Needles you cannot thread.

FRANCIS FRITH

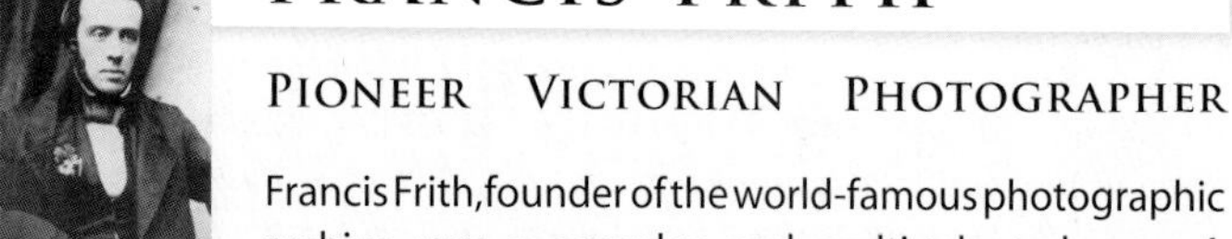

PIONEER VICTORIAN PHOTOGRAPHER

Francis Frith, founder of the world-famous photographic archive, was a complex and multi-talented man. A devout Quaker and a highly successful Victorian businessman, he was philosophical by nature and pioneering in outlook. By 1855 he had already established a wholesale grocery business in Liverpool, and sold it for the astonishing sum of £200,000, which is the equivalent today of over £15,000,000. Now in his thirties, and captivated by the new science of photography, Frith set out on a series of pioneering journeys up the Nile and to the Near East.

INTRIGUE AND EXPLORATION

He was the first photographer to venture beyond the sixth cataract of the Nile. Africa was still the mysterious 'Dark Continent', and Stanley and Livingstone's historic meeting was a decade into the future. The conditions for picture taking confound belief. He laboured for hours in his wicker dark-room in the sweltering heat of the desert, while the volatile chemicals fizzed dangerously in their trays. Back in London he exhibited his photographs and was 'rapturously cheered' by members of the Royal Society. His reputation as a photographer was made overnight.

VENTURE OF A LIFE-TIME

By the 1870s the railways had threaded their way across the country, and Bank Holidays and half-day Saturdays had been made obligatory by Act of Parliament. All of a sudden the working man and his family were able to enjoy days out, take holidays, and see a little more of the world.

With typical business acumen, Francis Frith foresaw that these new tourists would enjoy having souvenirs to commemorate their days out. For the next thirty years he travelled the country by train and by pony and trap, producing fine photographs of seaside resorts and beauty spots that were keenly bought by millions of Victorians. These prints were painstakingly pasted into family albums and pored over during the dark nights of winter, rekindling precious memories of summer excursions. Frith's studio was soon supplying retail shops all over the country, and by 1890 F Frith & Co had become the greatest specialist photographic publishing company in the world, with over 2,000 sales outlets, and pioneered the picture postcard.

FRANCIS FRITH'S LEGACY

Francis Frith had died in 1898 at his villa in Cannes, his great project still growing. By 1970 the archive he created contained over a third of a million pictures showing 7,000 British towns and villages.

Frith's legacy to us today is of immense significance and value, for the magnificent archive of evocative photographs he created provides a unique record of change in the cities, towns and villages throughout Britain over a century and more. Frith and his fellow studio photographers revisited locations many times down the years to update their views, compiling for us an enthralling and colourful pageant of British life and character.

We are fortunate that Frith was dedicated to recording the minutiae of everyday life. For it is this sheer wealth of visual data, the painstaking chronicle of changes in dress, transport, street layouts, buildings, housing and landscape that captivates us so much today, offering us a powerful link with the past and with the lives of our ancestors.

Computers have now made it possible for Frith's many thousands of images to be accessed almost instantly. The archive offers every one of us an opportunity to examine the places where we and our families have lived and worked down the years. Its images, depicting our shared past, are now bringing pleasure and enlightenment to millions around the world a century and more after his death.

For further information visit: www.francisfrith.com

INTERIOR DECORATION

Frith's photographs can be seen framed and as giant wall murals in thousands of pubs, restaurants, hotels, banks, retail stores and other public buildings throughout Britain. These provide interesting and attractive décor, generating strong local interest and acting as a powerful reminder of gentler days in our increasingly busy and frenetic world.

FRITH PRODUCTS

All Frith photographs are available as prints and posters in a variety of different sizes and styles. In the UK we also offer a range of other gift and stationery products illustrated with Frith photographs, although many of these are not available for delivery outside the UK – see our web site for more information on the products available for delivery in your country.

THE INTERNET

Over 100,000 photographs of Britain can be viewed and purchased on the Frith web site. The web site also includes memories and reminiscences contributed by our customers, who have personal knowledge of localities and of the people and properties depicted in Frith photographs. If you wish to learn more about a specific town or village you may find these reminiscences fascinating to browse. Why not add your own comments if you think they would be of interest to others? See **www.francisfrith.com**

PLEASE HELP US BRING FRITH'S PHOTOGRAPHS TO LIFE

Our authors do their best to recount the history of the places they write about. They give insights into how particular towns and villages developed, they describe the architecture of streets and buildings, and they discuss the lives of famous people who lived there. But however knowledgeable our authors are, the story they tell is necessarily incomplete.

Frith's photographs are so much more than plain historical documents. They are living proofs of the flow of human life down the generations. They show real people at real moments in history; and each of those people is the son or daughter of someone, the brother or sister, aunt or uncle, grandfather or grandmother of someone else. All of them lived, worked and played in the streets depicted in Frith's photographs.

We would be grateful if you would give us your insights into the places shown in our photographs: the streets and buildings, the shops, businesses and industries. Post your memories of life in those streets on the Frith website: what it was like growing up there, who ran the local shop and what shopping was like years ago; if your workplace is shown tell us about your working day and what the building is used for now. Read other visitors' memories and reconnect with your shared local history and heritage. With your help more and more Frith photographs can be brought to life, and vital memories preserved for posterity, and for the benefit of historians in the future.

Wherever possible, we will try to include some of your comments in future editions of our books. Moreover, if you spot errors in dates, titles or other facts, please let us know, because our archive records are not always completely accurate—they rely on 140 years of human endeavour and hand-compiled records. You can email us using the contact form on the website.

Thank you!

For further information, trade, or author enquiries please contact us at the address below:

The Francis Frith Collection, Oakley Business Park, Wylye Road, Dinton, Wiltshire SP3 5EU.

Tel: +44 (0)1722 716 376 Fax: +44 (0)1722 716 881

e-mail: sales@francisfrith.co.uk **www.francisfrith.com**